Creating and Driving Service Excellence

An Executive's Guide
to IT Service Management

Sharon Taylor

London: TSO

TSO
information & publishing solutions

Published by TSO (The Stationery Office) and available from:

Online
www.tsoshop.co.uk

Mail, Telephone, Fax and E-mail
TSO
PO Box 29, Norwich, NR3 1GN
Telephone orders/General enquiries: 0870 600 5522
Fax orders: 0870 600 5533
E-mail: customer.services@tso.co.uk
Textphone 0870 240 3701

TSO@Blackwell and other Accredited Agents

Published by The Stationery Office (TSO).

The information contained in this publication is believed to be correct at the time of manufacture. Whilst care has been taken to ensure that the information is accurate, the publisher can accept no responsibility for any errors or omissions or for changes to the details given.

ITIL® is a Registered Trade Mark of the Office of Government Commerce in the United Kingdom and other countries

COBIT® is a Registered Trade Mark of ISACA

CMMI® is a Registered Trade Mark of Carnegie Mellon University

TOGAF® is a registered trademark of The Open Group in the United States and other countries

VAL-IT™ is a trademark of ISACA

priSM® is a registered trademark of the IT Service Management Forum

RISK-IT is a registered trademark of ISACA

itSMF® is a registered trademark of the IT Service Management Forum

ISO is a registered trademark of the International Organization for Standardization

Cover image © Mikhail Mishchenko – Fotolia.com

A CIP catalogue record for this book is available from the British Library

A Library of Congress CIP catalogue record has been applied for

First published 2011

ISBN 9780117069022

Printed in the United Kingdom for The Stationery Office

P002452117   c10   09/11

Contents

Foreword

As a business executive, I doubt you would consider making a sizeable investment without having a vision for the outcomes you could achieve. I also doubt that you'd write a cheque for thousands of dollars without knowing what you'd get in return.

When it comes to IT service management, many organizations like yours have sadly done just that. Why? Because we know instinctively that IT is critical to our business and we have to have it, but we don't think much about how to manage it or the consequences to our business if it is not done properly ...until something goes wrong and your customers start to complain.

For over 20 years IT service management has been considered globally accepted best practice. The industry experts of this century agree on its value. Why then do some IT service management implementations fail to succeed?

Research reveals that executives in these organizations tend to consider IT service management an operational level issue and don't realize its strategic importance to business value and profitability. Some research also suggests that many executives don't provide support for IT service management initiatives and the cultural changes that are needed to sustain it simply because they don't see the strategic value.

IT service management is a strategic business asset; one that you can capitalize on as you would any other business asset. So, in other words, you need to pay attention to IT service management.

The reality, that has been proven over and over and over again, is that adopting IT service management can mean the difference between survival or extinction of an IT department and often the business itself. IT service management saves money. IT service management is what the best-performing companies in the world use to manage services. It's time you knew what they know.

I have seen the smallest and largest of companies begin an IT service management project and reap benefits they could never have imagined. I hope, with this work, to share this experience and help you reconsider the importance and relevance of IT service management to your company, so that you too can help IT fulfill the potential that is increasingly critical to any successful business.

I believe that one of the primary reasons executives have been mislead into thinking IT service management is just for IT is because everything ever written on the topic is full of IT jargon, slanted towards an IT audience.

This book is different. It is not IT jargon; it's business truths about why you need to seriously consider how important IT service management is to your business.

You can likely finish this book in the time it takes to commute from the office to your home. The insight and value you will find in these pages will last for many, many more miles.

1 A business imperative

The best way to understand the power of IT service management is to forget that it has any relationship to IT at all. Its purpose is to add value, stability and quality to business outcomes. The IT service management industry gets itself wound up around IT service management as a technology-enabled management practice when, in fact, it has more to do with making services useful to business than anything else. Actually, than *everything* else.

We forget the complexity that IT has woven into the simplest aspects of daily life. From the moment we wake up and put on coffee, we are indebted to technology to enable our lives. Our dependence on IT makes it a business imperative. The only time we actually stop to consider this is when something goes wrong...

On August 14, 2003, shortly after 2 P.M. Eastern Daylight Time, a high-voltage power line in northern Ohio brushed against some overgrown trees and shut down – a fault, as it's known in the power industry. The line had softened under the heat of the high current coursing through it. Normally, the problem would have tripped an alarm in the control room of FirstEnergy Corporation, an Ohio-based utility company, but the alarm system failed.

Over the next hour and a half, as system operators tried to understand what was happening, three other lines sagged into trees and switched off, forcing other power lines to shoulder an extra burden. Overtaxed, they cut out by 4:05 P.M., tripping a cascade of failures throughout Southeastern Canada and eight Northeastern states.

All told, 50 million people lost power for up to two days in the biggest blackout in North American history. The event contributed to at least 11 deaths and cost an estimated $6 billion.[1]

This was the result of something going wrong with IT.

IT service management may have prevented this situation from occurring. After investigating the cause, it was determined that the failure of the alarm systems (an IT service), and this not being noticed in time, was the catalyst for the events that followed. How would this company's Chief Executive Officer (CEO) have reacted knowing that using IT service management may have prevented such a disaster? This is an extreme example meant to drive home the point that IT service management isn't just about managing the small, everyday service issues. It has everything to do with ensuring that a small issue (like an alarm failure), is detected through sound service management practices, thus preventing larger, more costly issues.

If you think about your own organization, you can likely find examples of business disruption caused by IT failures. They don't have to be full-blown disasters to be costly. Even short disruptions to services during times of critical business activity are enough to create significant issues with costly consequences. You can likely find many more of these than you should. The costs of these failures are staggering and most companies have no idea what that cost actually is.

---

1   The 2003 Northeast Blackout – Five years later, JR Minkel, August 13 2008, published by Scientific American

A successful business is a profitable one. Profit can be in the form of money, achieving mandates, meeting expectations and delivering quality products and services. In every case, no matter how your business defines its value, the only way to sustain it is to balance cost and risk, with competitiveness and distinction.

Preserving business profitability, ensuring quality and value for IT services is the warranty we get from IT service management. In many companies the use of IT service management practices is considered a business imperative and they will mandate IT service management capability be demonstrated by any supplier of IT services. The standards industry also recognizes the value of IT service management and has created formal compliance standards for many IT service aspects such as governance, management systems and security.

It is estimated by independent research organizations that using IT service management can provide a rate of Return on Investment (ROI) of about 40% in 18 months[1]. Moreover, IT service management pays for itself in fewer than 12 months in many cases. Why would any executive ignore a perfectly good opportunity to save money, protect business investment and provide quality service?

Those who know about IT service management don't.

So what *is* IT service management?

Simply, IT service management is a collection of best practices, frameworks, standards, methods, attitudes, behaviour and cultures used to monitor, measure and manage IT services. Their objectives are to meet business needs for flexible, reliable, sustainable and cost effective IT services.

Now, more importantly, why should you care?

2   Cases in point

Before we get into more detail about what IT service management is, lets briefly look at what it has accomplished for some.

Every year, case studies are published about the use of IT service management practices and the Return on Investment it accomplishes through cost savings, process efficiencies, risk avoidance, compliance and better service quality. Let's have the evidence speak for itself:

Industry Sector	ROI For IT service management Adoption
Financial Services	
Capital One[2]	• 92% reduction in critical service incidents • 20% savings in overall IT support costs
Visa[3]	75% improvement in monitoring of system outages
JP Morgan Chase[4]	• 93% customer satisfaction rate • decrease service calls by 500,000

---

2   Computerworld, CIO.com

3   Smart Enterprise Magazine

4   Computerworld, UK

Industry Sector	ROI For IT service management Adoption
Manufacturing	
Johnson & Johnson[5]	• $30 million in savings for process renewal • average help desk incident resolution down from 27 minutes to 18 minutes
Procter and Gamble[6]	• 8% reduction in operating costs ($125 million per annum) • 10% reduction in overall IT budget
Shell Oil[7]	• 6,000 staff days reduced and $5 million saved annually
Telecommunications	
Avaya[8]	• Reduced IT budget by 30%
Government	
Ontario, Canada[9]	Reduced support costs by 40%

These are not extreme examples. They are common ones and every size of organization has had positive results. Bear in mind that every cost reduction or service target improvement shown in the above examples, translates also into business benefits. Overall organizational costs are reduced, risk to the business is reduced and service quality to the customer is improved. This is NOT just about IT savings. This is about business savings.

This should make you care about why IT service management is important to you.

---

5   Ascendant Ventures

6   Network World

7   Smart Enterprise Magazine

8   Techworld

9   Network World

3 Business leaders speak IT service management

 Most Executives have become recession weary and managing costs is an ingredient in just about every conversation a Chief Executive has. IT staff to user ratios have been gutted, projects and initiatives have been cancelled, and budgets have been slashed. What isn't recession weary are customer expectations. The only way to meet expectations is to ignite capacity with services that conserve costs while expanding the arsenal of capability. This is innovation. How?

Each year, surveys of Chief Executives around the world agree on what their priorities are in order to exist in the current recovering economic climate and meet increasing business demands. Each year, those priorities don't change much.

1. Attract new and retain existing customers

2. Grow revenues

3. Improve business processes and effectiveness

4. Encourage the business/IT partnership

5. Control costs

6. Drive business innovation

7. Support compliance and managing risk

8. Create market differentiation

9.   Refine business strategy

10.   IT value delivery

These top business priorities all have a common characteristic. **Every one of them is exactly what IT service management practices exist for.** Amazingly, despite the existence of IT service management as a respected and proven set of best practices, companies who may not have heard of it, or miss seeing its full potential, will take other paths to try and achieve these initiatives and some of them will spend countless hours and dollars trying to reinvent a wheel which already has a well refined tread – IT service management.

IT service management applied to the top business priorities

Let's look at how IT service management has helped some businesses to meet these top priorities:

1.   Attract new and retain existing customers

"When we adopted IT service management, we learned how to engage the business in a meaningful dialogue that we both understood. This allowed us to work with the business as our partner and define what business outcomes we needed to enable and what services could achieve this. Not only did we learn what services we needed to provide, BUT ALSO what made them invaluable to the business both in function and performance. There is no price tag for us on how much value our ability to positively impact business success in a tangible, measured way has."
CIO, global publishing company

IT service management practices are designed to ensure that IT services support tangible and defined business outcomes. Customer growth and retention ranks among these. Among the IT service practices I've used with this customer to grow its customer base are:

- Defining and capturing market spaces – using this IT service management practice can help redefine a business's true market potential. This area of practice takes a business through the steps of seeing where IT capabilities can be used to attract new customers. Business leaders can easily not notice that IT services can uncover new business opportunities.

- Using a service portfolio[10] and catalogue[11] to market services – service portfolios and catalogues are a long-standing part of IT service management. Business customers can often utilize the existing platforms of IT to create similar business-facing portfolios and catalogues for their customers in addition to the benefits that managing IT services and investments have through portfolio and catalogue management.

- Enabling faster time to market for business products and services – This is a magnificent benefit of IT service management for the business. using IT service management practices such as

---

10   'Portfolio' refers to a service portfolio, which is the practice of managing services as a group of value-producing assets which are holistically managed with a view to overall ROI, investment and business value. More information on service portfolio management can be found in the ITIL framework (see further reading reference section).

11   'Catalog or Catalogue' refers to an ITIL process *Service catalogue management* and is about listing the IT services available to the business with details about each. A service catalogue has different views, some for the business and some more technical for IT to see how IT assets are joined up in the provision of a service.

change, release and deployment, testing, etc. helps to minimize the risks and costs for producing new products and services (not only IT ones) and can achieve faster cycle times for a competitive business edge.

- Reducing business risk and enabling innovation – IT service management practices help business to understand the relative risks they face and how best to mitigate these. Business decisions are often made with more justification when the true risks are known.

- Creating new product-enabling services – There are few business products today that are not in some way enabled by technology. Creating a solid business and IT partnership nurtures collaboration about how IT can help innovate new products and services and, of course, how IT service management will help ensure they are reliable and manageable.

IT service management helps promote a partnership between the business and IT by ensuring that every service delivered by IT is measured in business value. When IT understands the business you are in, it can use its technology expertise to offer up IT innovations that can help capture new business markets and produce business products faster, all helping businesses to attract and retain customers.

2.   Grow Revenues

"Our IT organization built its IT service management adoption business case around IT efficiency improvements and cost reductions. That alone was enough to satisfy such a mandate since IT costs were consuming a larger percentage of our overall budget with each passing year. An unexpected outcome for us was the better

> *understanding of our core business that IT*
> *matured toward and the ideas for new products*
> *and cheaper ways to produce existing products*
> *that IT helped enable. This increased business*
> *revenues significantly and that trend has continued.*
> *Now it's an embedded expectation of the success*
> *of IT service management in our company."*
> CEO Plastics Manufacturing company

Releasing business profit is often a by-product of IT service management through the cost reductions, gains through better quality, efficiency and effectiveness of IT services. Enabling business growth through product innovation and increased competitiveness is achieved by:

- **Lowering** total cost of service ownership – Many companies don't really know the true cost of IT services. IT service management helps to define, measure and contain these costs through common processes, procedures and performance monitoring. We think of costs as the ones we can tangibly account for. IT service management helps us to see the intangible costs as well and see how to manage them effectively.

- **Identifying** improvements that inspire product and service innovations – When you know what is possible using the assets you already pay for, new products and services can often be achieved by exploiting existing assets. This lowers the cost of services even further by spreading fixed costs across a greater range of assets.

- **Reducing** risk to the business and increasing the safety margin of transformational business changes – Dynamically changing business needs are a staple in the IT service management diet. The expertise of reducing risks and the unnecessary costs of uncontrolled service outages means that IT service management helps minimize risk AND cost.

3. Improving business processes and effectiveness

"Our customer satisfaction was consistently poor because the perception of our ability to provide value was low. Until we applied IT service management practices and gained control of the IT service stability and consistent customer management, we were reactive and ad-hoc in most things we did. IT service management not only lowered our overall cost of ownership, we immediately saw an improvement in system performance, operational management and the customers saw it too. Satisfaction ratings soared and costs went down".

CIO, Auto manufacturing company

IT service management improves these areas by imposing stabilized controls and monitoring against pre-defined expectations. Process-driven actions, skilled resources that are appropriately trained and measurable results are the mechanisms that achieve this. Typical outputs seen by the business are:

- Improved support response
- Services that function and perform as expected (service utility & warranty)
- Reduced costs of service provision
- Meaningful service reports
- Less firefighting and fixing the same issues repeatedly

- Proactive monitoring, correction and preventative service maintenance
- Trained workforce

These outcomes lead to satisfied customers of IT because they are seeing responsive, professional, consistent service from the IT organization.

4. Encouraging the business/IT partnership

> *"Pre-ITSM, our organization did not see any value in having IT represented in corporate strategic planning meetings. The CEO was not convinced that IT was competent to understand business drivers, market conditions that affected them and how IT could enable better business profitability. Post-ITSM, our core competences and service improvement innovations delivered tangible business value that we could measure and prove to the Corporate Board. IT now has a seat on the Board."*
>
> IT Director, Aerospace Company

IT service management practices illustrate the professional abilities of IT to the business customer. The use of process-driven monitoring, control and improvements open doors for IT executives to be part of the strategic development and planning for the business. This engenders a true partnership and customer loyalty to IT. Examples of some of the areas of IT service management practice that can illustrate the cooperative partnership are:

- **Mature Service Portfolio management** – This practice takes an investment view approach and considers business and IT assets as having potential value-creating possibilities. This requires

IT be in on the ground floor of strategic business decision-making and is a reflection of a true partnership approach.

- **IT strategic planning** – This has to take into account the corporate strategy and business directions. IT strategy cannot be done in a vacuum of IT. By demonstrating with the IT strategy, the business value that will be realized, the business customer can see the danger of NOT having IT at the corporate table.

- **Service Catalogue management** – Some of my customers have enjoyed an unexpected benefit of re-selling some of their IT services to their end customers. Looking at IT services through a catalogue view can often uncover hidden potential like this. Using the technology that enables an IT service catalogue as the platform for a business customer online catalogue enhances business service offerings and reduces cost to market by exploiting existing assets. This is a good example of a true business/IT collaborative partnership.

- **Standards compliance** – Whether you need to comply with legislation like Sarbanes-Oxley[12] or quality standard like ISO9001[13], IT service management helps position your business and IT organizations to use IT service management frameworks to achieve standards compliance. IT

12 Sarbanes-Oxley refers to the US Sarbanes-Oxley Act passed into US law in 2002. Its intent is to protect investors by improving the accuracy and reliability of corporate disclosures made pursuant to the securities laws, and for other purposes.

13 ISO 9001 refers to the international standard of quality management as defined by the International Organization for Standardization.

service management practices are designed to align to many common standards, so doing one helps achieve the other.

- **Audit reporting** – Most of our IT services rely on a chain of supply that includes third parties. Using IT service management as part of your overall strategy can help ensure that you include audit frameworks as part of managing your supply chain effectively. This lowers risk, ensures consistent use of practice and increases customer confidence in responsible IT management.

- **Continual improvement plans** – Every service provider aspires to improve and mature over time. Cost efficiencies, quality improvements and better management can be enabled with IT service management. Continual improvement is a basic tenet of IT service management. Whether it's small changes to a process or procedure, or the addition of an entire process or practice, these all add up to significant savings and improved service quality for the business customer.

5. Controlling costs

"When we decided to adopt IT service management the main driver was the promise of reducing costs in order to meet budget cuts. I will admit to being sceptical of the claims about how IT service management would impact costs. The ROI for us was about 200% within the first year and has risen steadily since. We actually try to downplay our cost reduction successes to avoid further budget reductions! For us, IT service management did make the difference."
CIO, pharmaceutical testing company

As a significant contributor to managing and lowering IT costs, IT service management provides the capacity to accurately calculate costs of services, measure and report on them and lower costs through improvements. Over 60% of companies do not know the true cost of IT services. IT service management changes that by:

- Using techniques that accurately cost IT services and uncover hidden and intangible costs
- Monitoring and tracking costs that are tied to services and value, not simply accounting items
- Using predictive analysis to understand IT service costs in ROI and VOI (Value of Investment) terms
- Using value-mapping to reduce waste and reinvest in value-add activities
- Reducing time to market, cost of changes, and support overheads

6.   Driving business innovation

> *"We always believed that only we [the business] knew what was best for our customers. Our IT service providers proved that, by using their experience with IT, they could help us reinvent our products and services to exceed our own expectations, those of our customers and especially those of our competitors. We now make it a regular event to collaborate with IT when planning our market strategies."*
> CEO, Telecommunications Company

IT service management heightens the awareness of the dependence on IT services the business has in order to do its job. A by-product is the acute awareness by IT of the business processes enabled by them. The customer-centric view IT service management provides, allows for innovation from IT to be embedded in service thinking and this is a well-documented benefit. Some ways this has been applied are:

- Using a service portfolio to initiate collaborative business service planning and tying that to new technologies and innovative uses of existing technologies
- Tying profitability to service designs and new ideas for business services
- Leveraging improved IT architectures for business models, such as cloud computing, to increase business service reach and range
- Using IT services, like a service catalogue to host business to customer solutions

7. Supporting compliance and managing risk

"During the economic meltdown of 2008, our bank needed to rethink how we approached compliance and risk management. It was evident that the IT department provided a key piece of the puzzle since our services are largely driven electronically. We had already begun to invest in standards and risk profiling for services and this put us ahead of the curve in defining new models to stabilize our business risk and meet new government legislated compliance."
CIO, USA Bank conglomerate

CIOs are facing new opportunities for addressing risk and compliance through business models that can spread risk and measure compliance across the supply chain. IT service management frameworks provide knowledge for determining the optimal structures for risk tolerance and compliance rigor:

- Using ITIL[14] (IT Infrastructure Library) service models to determine the optimal risk tolerance and compliance requirements
- Using ITIL Service Design to define the service criteria that considers the risk and compliance needs, within the design aspects
- Using Risk-IT framework to develop your evaluation criteria for risk governance
- Using ISO standards and requiring their use within your supply chain to address specific areas of compliance needs

8. Create market differentiation

> *"Our company was tendering for the network service provision with the largest potential customer we ever had. We won that business and have kept it for 5 years now. Our customer told us that it was our commitment to IT service management practices that set us apart from our competitors because we could prove our value in business terms and show how we could improve their business success. To our customers, that was a primary and strategic requirement in an IT provider."*

CIO, managed services company.

With so many service provider choices in the market, internal or external IT organizations must demonstrate their value and what sets them apart from the competition. The fact that you use IT service management practices alone can be a differentiator by:

---

14 ITIL and ITIL Service Design refers to an ITSM framework. Please see Further reading section at the end of this book for a further details on the ITIL framework.

- Demonstrating you understand that supporting business outcomes *IS* the goal, not the by-product
- Being able to quantify in measurable terms, how your services add to the business' bottom line
- Providing a consistent customer quality experience through repeatable process use
- Using industry recognized practices that integrate with those of customers and others in the supply chain

9. Refining business strategy

A common ailment of dysfunctional business/IT collaboration is the translation of needs between each party. IT expects the business to be adept at articulating what their service needs are, but business doesn't understand IT. As a result, business strategies don't always end up being useful for IT as a basis to understand needs. Worse, the lack of common understanding can prompt the business to overstate their needs in an effort to avoid services that don't measure up. IT service management helps balance the equation by helping both parties to work through the identification of service needs in a language that both speak and understand, such as:

- **Defining the meaning of service** – This is an invaluable element for setting expectations and service needs. The IT provider understands what a service means to the business and the business understands what they are asking for from IT. This is a win-win formula
- **The use of IT service management positions an IT provider to know emerging technology innovations that can help refine business strategy for competitive edge** – Businesses whose

IT providers practice IT service management trust them to help guide and refine business strategy because they have proven they understand the business and its needs

- **Using service Portfolio and demand management along with VAL-IT and Risk-IT** – This can help guide a business through strategic decisions by understanding investment implications, value and risks before they commit to a strategic direction

> *"During the past 3 years we have had mature IT service management practices in place, the business has seen many ways we have helped them to innovate new ideas to achieve their goals, while saving money and advancing their technology to current, less expensive solutions. They now rely on us to provide strategic advice and they place a high importance on how IT can help them achieve their goals."*
> IT Manager, Public Sector Government

10. IT Value delivery

> *"Even though we had a good relationship with our business customers, neither of us really could articulate the value IT provided in a meaningful way. This made it hard to convince senior management, our Chief Financial Officer and the key decision-makers to keep investing in IT to allow us to mature further and provide greater value. As we learned more about IT service management and began using frameworks like ITIL, COBIT, TOGAF, Six Sigma and Lean practices, we found it so much easier to define value in business terms, back it up with metrics and evidence of improving value. The decision-*

makers no longer question IF we provide value. They now ask IT's advice on how they can improve theirs!"

IT Manager, National Retail chain

This one is listed tenth, not because it's the least important, but because it needs to stick out and be remembered as you read further. There are too many reasons to list here that support why IT must be able to demonstrate value in delivery of its services. The fact that every supplier is optional for a customer should be reason enough. IT service management frameworks share the commonness of being focused on customer needs, business alignment, service-centric and centred on enabling business outcomes. The use of IT service management across the globe reinforces its ability to create value, to demonstrate how IT provides value and, most importantly, to deliver value consistently, measurably and cost effectively. Specific areas which focus hard evidence for this are:

- ITIL service strategy for creating business value outcome statements that tie tangible metrics to performance

- ITIL financial management for determining the Return on Investment for services and cost of utilization that can be monitored for positive or negative change over recurring cycles

- Val-IT for determining how to utilize business investments and service assets to be maximized by IT through their economic lifecycle

- Using IT service management frameworks to build an understanding of what customers value and how to translate that into services which enable that value.

4　What's in IT service management for you?

If meeting the expectations of the priorities listed in the previous section is not enough to convince you that IT service management warrants your attention, what follows should seal the deal.

Some of the largest companies in the world have become the poster organizations for how IT service management can be transformational, not only to the IT organization but to the entire company. There are just as many examples of success in medium and small companies.

The basic concepts within IT service management of governance, strategy, management and execution practices are adaptable outside of an IT context as well, and the business world has some shining examples of IT service management used in non-IT environments. The following list of benefits is written from an IT service provision perspective, but you are encouraged to think outside the box and consider their uses in non-IT contexts as well.

Benefits

Investment control

 Many executives feel that IT service costs are mostly overhead with no measurable return on investment. IT service management experts will position these frameworks as critically linked to ROI. The truth is somewhere in the middle. There is no debate that IT service management not only allows you to determine your IT costs and measure ROI, but it allows you to manipulate ROI and VOI intentionally and with accuracy. How? By understanding IT costs and revenue generating opportunities accurately. IT service management has proven its ability to lower IT costs significantly.

Improved customer satisfaction

 Business customers being disillusioned with IT service is a serious and all too common issue. The root cause of this is often a bit too much he said–she said without measurable performance information to back it up. Downtime that is recurring, without a solution in sight, and the lack of understanding of the needs of either side creates a sense of distrust and angst among customers and destabilizes the morale and relationship between provider and customer.

The flip side of this scenario is overinflated customer expectations fuelled by inconsistent service experiences; service levels which are not agreed and the heroism of firefighting the same issues without resolving the underlying problems. The IT providers can unwittingly set unrealistic customer expectations and then fail to consistently achieve them, leaving the customers feeling underserved, even though they may be getting exactly the level of service they pay for. IT service management enables a method for setting service levels that are measurable and consistently achievable and, therefore, improve customer satisfaction. The level of service need not be over the top, but if it is consistent, and within agreed levels, customers will actually be more satisfied with services that cost less to provide than sporadic, unpredictable quality.

Improved customer loyalty

It might surprise you to realize that consumer behaviour is mostly predictable. Customers will be loyal to companies and brands that serve their needs, make them feel valued and that provide a consistent consumer experience. IT service management provides an IT organization with the structure, discipline, methods and techniques that build the kind of stability, consistency and demonstration of value that customers are loyal to. Something as simple as well-scripted service desk agents that have access to customer profile information can vastly improve the comfort level of customers by knowing their service desk knows them and what services they use, thus saving the customer time and making them feel valued. IT service management frameworks are centred on value to the business and customer satisfaction, loyalty and retention stem from this.

Attracting new customers

Companies spend large sums on marketing, hoping to attract new customers. This is one of a valuable set of tools to create new business. IT service management is another because it transforms IT organizations into high performing, responsive, service-intuitive and reliable service providers. Because IT service management has become widely known, many customers will require compliance to IT service management standards and practices before they will engage in discussions for potential business. Marketing IT service management as one of your strengths is instantly recognizable in the service provider marketplace and should be one of your tools for attracting new customers.

Influencing business decisions

 IT organizations that invest in best practices become trusted, influential and relied upon to contribute to business success by helping create it. IT service management positions IT organizations to be considered among the most strategic influencers of business decisions. Those who invest in frameworks across the IT service management layers are well versed in strategic planning, understand the value of IT to business profitability and can participate in business strategic planning as a valued and trusted partner to the business.

Lowering cost of ownership

 This is an area of attention that never gets old. It's also the single, largest reason most companies undertake IT service management implementation to this day. Industry average experiences with IT service management results boast lower cost of ownership as a major advantage, along with surprisingly short ROI for the effort.

Supply chain control

Over the past decade the number and types of service providers, and service provision models have increased dramatically. So too has the complexity of managing the supply chain. IT service management practices have evolved to the point that they are no longer a question of 'if' they are needed but 'when and how'. When it comes to supply chain management, IT service management's value is unchallenged in the industry. Because integration and harmony of the many parts of the supply chain are critical to value and quality for the customer, IT service management practices make it possible to manage complex layers of supply and demand from an end to end perspective and not just as constituent parts. IT service management covers everything from how the supply chain players need to meet standards of compliance, risk profiles, practice disciplines, to performance incentives and penalty sanctions.

Proactive demand management[15]

Nothing will drive up IT service costs faster than unexpected fluctuations in demand. Underused capacity is expensive and unnecessary if IT service management practices include proactive demand management. A lack of capacity will result in business service disruption with the type of fallout no IT executive can sustain – loss

---

15 'Demand management' is a process within ITIL that is focused on understanding how the business uses services, monitoring the patterns and trends and using that knowledge to ensure IT services have the capacity to meet demand as it changes and predicting future business needs.

of reputation for IT quality, lack of trust, cost to both IT and business, etc. IT service management lifecycle practices from all the frameworks mentioned in this publication can eliminate this from ever occurring in your organization and for far less cost than you'd expect.

Strategic asset management

 A consistent and predictable failure in IT service provision is the underuse of assets. This stems from the approach most non-IT service management organizations take to new service ventures. Some very common mistakes are things such as thinking that redundancy is the best way to assure service availability. That is usually only the case in extremes now that other technical innovations such as virtualization, cloud computing and the like have come into being. What happens is that organizations fail to systematically evaluate asset usage options and tie that process thinking into all aspect of planning, design, and architecture when looking forward. IT service management practices engender this mindset within the execution of processes and this is one area where costs for providing service and asset management benefits yield immediate results.

There are many more benefits and reasons to adopt IT service management, but this should be enough to compel you to take IT service management seriously. You will be in good company.

Some of the better-known companies who use and have benefitted from IT service management are:

Procter and Gamble	NASA	Barclays
Boeing	Pfizer	DHL
Xcel	UPS	Hitachi
Caterpillar	Sony	Toyota
General Motors	Thomson-Reuters	Lockheed Martin

5 IT service management today

Management is a term that is overused and misunderstood. As a simple, uniformly understood concept, management is about getting people to accomplish desired goals and objectives efficiently and effectively. Whether you put 'business or IT' in front of that sentence, it is still correct. There is a direct relationship to successful businesses and how well they 'manage'.

The story only begins there. Business and IT are both judged by their customers not on how they 'manage' but by the quality and value produced through the act of managing.

IT service management is built upon the basic elements of a quality management system.

1. **Customer focused** – Organizations depend on customers and must understand current and future customer needs, should meet customer requirements and strive to exceed customer expectations.

2. **Leadership** – Leaders establish unity of purpose and direction for an organization. They should create and maintain an environment in which people can become fully involved in achieving the organization's objectives.

3. **People** – People at every level are the essence of an organization and their involvement enables their capabilities to be used as assets for the organization's benefit.

4. **Process** – A desired result is achieved more efficiently when activities and related resources are managed as a process

5. **System** – Identifying, understanding and managing interrelated processes as a system contributes to the organization's effectiveness and efficiency in achieving its objectives

6. **Improvement** – Continual improvement of the organization's overall performance should be a permanent objective of the organization

7. **Decision-making** – Effective decisions are based on the analysis of data, information, knowledge and wisdom

8. **Relationships** – An organization and its suppliers are interdependent and a mutually beneficial relationship enhances the ability of both to create value and profitability

The IT industry adapted these basic principles within the IT service management approach and has developed and refined best management practices within specific bodies of knowledge. These work in synergy to create a portfolio of service management capabilities. Let's explore how this is structured for IT service management.

IT Management System

Figure 1 IT service management structure

Best practices within quality management systems are organized to address management concerns at various levels within the organization.

Governance – The overarching corporate policy and direction-setting level. Vision for the organizational objectives are formed within this area of control.

Strategy – Program, fiscal and organizational structures direction-setting layer. This is where the cultural tone and human dynamics are established through example and practice.

Management – Process and operational policy-setting layer. This is where vision, strategy, controls and cultures are cultivated, reinforced and monitored.

Execution – Procedural and work instruction operational layer. This is where practice, use and critical innovative thinking are applied and organizational evolution occurs.

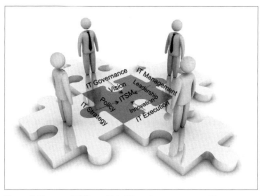

Figure 2 Responsibilities within IT service management layers

In terms of a 'system' we think of these layers as a cyclical, interrelated lifecycle flow of capabilities, practices, behaviours, outcomes and hindsight. This 'lifecycle' flow is seen in most IT service management frameworks.

This is supported by the evolution of IT service management thought leadership, which has kept pace with how technologies have evolved to be more tightly aligned to business value. This evolution is illustrated in the following diagram:

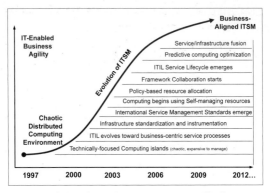

Figure 3 Evolution of IT service management toward business alignment

From among the many bodies of knowledge, and their respective frameworks, there are subsets that have captured the forefront of mainstream IT service management best practice.

Figure 4 Structural positioning of IT service management frameworks

This publication will focus on a key subset of these as a good base for IT service management:

- International Organization for Standardization (ISO[2]) – A collection of standards related to IT service management and quality management systems. Specifically the following standards are generally accepted as mainstream:
    - ISO 15504 series – Software Process Improvement and Capability Determination
    - ISO 20000 series – Service Management System
    - ISO 38500 – IT Governance
    - ISO 27000 series – IT Security
    - ISO 9000 series – Quality Management
    - ISO 19770 – Software Asset Management
- Control Objectives for Information and related Technology (COBIT) – An IT Governance and strategy framework for IT governance and audit
- ITIL Service Management (ITIL) – An IT service management best practice framework for IT strategy, design, transition, operation and improvement
- Technical Open Group Architectural Framework (TOGAF) – A strategy and management framework for IT architecture
- Capability Maturity Model for Information (CMMI) – An assessment framework for IT practice maturity
- VAL-IT – A strategic and management framework for mapping IT value investments to business priorities
- RISK-IT – An evaluation framework for assessing risk tolerance and positioning for IT

- Six Sigma – A control framework for detecting and eliminating defects
- eTOM – A best practice framework used primarily in the telecommunications industry and similar to ITIL in construct

(More complete details about these frameworks is included in the references and further reading section at the end of this publication as Appendix A.)

You will have noticed by now that there is some overlap and that frameworks can fit into more than one management layer. The following table positions each of the frameworks within its predominant layers.

Table 1 provides a general level of clarity about where these frameworks fit in relation to one another.

What makes these frameworks similar is their structure. They are all built around policy, process, procedure and instruction. This stems from a common underlying concept for quality management, created by Dr. Deming[16], and promotes a central theme of Planning (What you will do), Doing (executing the plan), Checking (assessing how well its working) and Acting (making course corrections and improvements). Within the IT service management industry, this quality cycle is referred to as the PDCA cycle. Standards, best practices and methods all use this simple construct as the basis for IT service management.

---

16   Deming, W. Edwards (1986). *Out of the Crisis*. MIT Center for Advanced Engineering Study.

Table 1 Organization of frameworks by structural layer

ITSM Layer/ Framework	ISO (Standards)	COBIT (Audit)	VAL-IT (Investment)	TOGAF (Architecture)	Risk-IT (Risk Tolerance)	ITIL (Strategic Planning, Design, Delivery And Support)	Lean IT (Waste Reduction)	Six Sigma (Defect Controls)
Governance								
Strategy								
Management								
Execution								

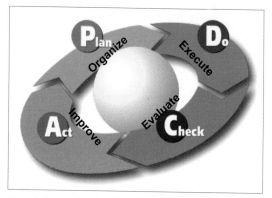

Figure 5 Deming Plan, Do, Check, Act cycle

Another common theme is that each of these frameworks is support by professionally recognized certifications, some for individual professional credentialing and others geared to organizations. Increasingly, IT service management is growing as a recognized profession supported by accredited qualification schemes. The demonstration of a workforce skilled in professionally recognized IT service management qualifications, and organizationally certified to IT service management compliance standards, often now factors into the decision for hiring resources or providers.

The itSMF International recognizes a number of these in a credentialing scheme called priSM (Professional Recognition in IT Service Management – www.theprisminstitute.org). More information about the various recognized framework qualifications can be found here.

As the IT service management industry matures and new bodies of knowledge emerge, there is a propensity to create more current versions of best practice and more overlap is becoming common. This creates a bit of a conundrum for the consumer of best practices to know which to use or not and how they overlap.

Do you need all of these?

Experts agree that the best approach is to consider a blend of the best from among the available in terms of meeting your needs. It is important to ensure that whatever approach you choose, that over time all of the structural areas be covered. Every IT organization should have elements within their IT service management framework that covers IT governance, IT strategy, IT process and procedure along with planned periodic assessment for maturity and improvement. This ensures a robust IT service management program.

Incidentally, this is the main reason that most of the highly successful organizations use a blended approach that will address their needs within each key structural area of governance, strategy, management and execution in their IT service management portfolio. Your portfolio does not need to include all or any of these, but why reinvent your own when best practices exist that are adaptable, scalable and proven?

Beware, though, of marketing hype. It really is just a matter of opinion about which of these is superior or better than the other. You need to consider them within the context of your needs.

6 Taking a practical approach to IT service management

By now, you have a good appreciation for the importance and value of having IT service management on your radar. The real test is actually making the choice to adopt it. Many books have already been written on the intricacies of implementation and there is no need to duplicate that effort here. The references section will provide additional recommended reading for the fine points of adopting, implementing and operating IT service management. Here, we will extract the basics for how to go about it.

Where to start

If you ask five people this question, you'll get five different answers. They all have merit. In the IT service management industry you'll find everything from self-proclaimed evangelists, experts, pundits and sceptics. Each will have a different view of how a company should approach IT service management, if at all. There really isn't one specific size for all, but there are some good questions to ask yourself that point you in the right direction.

First, accept that you really are already vested in IT service management to some degree. The nature of IT services is that, despite the lack of a formal IT service management program, you still have to meet the demands of:

Customers	Legislation	Security
Services	Changes	Requests
Incidents	Inventory	Facilities
Attitudes	Shareholders	Reporting
Perceptions	Health & Safety	Complaints
Expectations	Audits	Suppliers

All of these things are addressed as part of an IT service management program and the best place to start is to look at how well you manage these things today. The previous list is not exhaustive, but within it, there will be areas of strength and weakness and, perhaps, differing opinions on which are which. Give some thought to what your list is and where your strengths and weaknesses are. The ideal IT service management approach is to build on existing strengths (your own best practices) and improve in the weaker areas.

Next, after having read thus far, use your new understanding of the main types of IT service management frameworks.

Answer the following questions:

1. Do we understand our customers?

2. Have we agreed with the business on the definition of a 'service'?

3. Do our customers believe our quality of service is good.enough?

4. Can we identify the business processes we must support?

5. Do we know how much our services cost?

6. Do we know how much it costs the business when services fail?

7. Do we measure IT service performance in business terms?

8. Can we produce proof of our value to the business?

9. If we were not here, doing what we do, would the business fail?

10. Do we know our risk tolerance level and are we aligned to that today?

If you answered NO to any of these you are doing less than you need to in order to survive as the IT service provider of choice over the long term and IT service management is your way to change the answers to 'YES'.

Sit down with an IT service management expert (look inside your organization for experts too) and discuss options for adopting IT service management that will accomplish these four things:

1. Address some immediate concerns that demonstrate why adopting IT service management practices are a good thing for the entire organization. This builds acceptance and momentum.

2.   Create a plan for moving forward over months and years. This shows systematic thinking about how to address important issues incrementally, with proper planning and resources and recognition of an ongoing cycle of practices coming into play.

3.   Realize that IT service management is a journey as well as a destination and the learning and needs will evolve continually, as will your IT service management needs. Leave room to accept there will be room to improve.

4.   Understand that even a little change can make a large difference when it comes to IT service management adoption. Look for evidence within your own industry. It's there. There is no right or wrong approach, but there are a vast number of experiences out there that will help you choose your right way.

You know what IT service management is and what its worth...

But what will it cost?

7 The cost of using IT service management

If anyone were to tell you that there is little cost for using IT service management, you should be wary. There are costs associated with any IT service management program that you should be prepared for. What is just as important to consider, along with the cost, is what you save and how most IT service management programs end up paying for themselves through savings elsewhere.

Basic IT service management costs are made up of one-time and recurring costs. The best expert advice you will ever get is not to short-change ANY particular area. Plan over a reasonable time to have a balanced IT service management framework in your organization. An unbalanced IT service management program will suffer from a lack of overall effectiveness that can question the entire investment over time and reduce maximum ROI. Costs, by the way, are the same types whether you are implementing a small part of IT service management or larger parts. The costs have been portrayed here within the categories that we see most often with IT service management:

- People – This includes your organization's staff (both business and IT) and industry specialists who may be needed initially, and occasionally thereafter, for specific purposes.

- Processes – the actual IT service management practices themselves. They are referred to as 'processes' since that is what they most often are within IT service management, but this is intended to include all elements of IT service management practices.

- Products – the tools used to automate and execute processes within IT service management frameworks. These can include occasional tools such as those for conducting planning, audit, gap or maturity analysis or the daily-use tools for process execution such as incident, change, reporting and other operational processes.
- Partners – These include the supply chain that you may have that becomes a part of, or results from, adopting IT service management practices. Some examples are: Service Desk providers, Tool providers, outsource suppliers, managed services, etc.

One-time costs

The initial IT service management costs are not much different from many other first time initiative costs:

People

Bringing in temporary skilled resources to help plan and implement IT service management practices. Experts will include consultants, tool providers, commodity knowledge and technical suppliers. You will need to build organizational roles to own and manage IT service management. This means costs to train, certify or otherwise skill your workforce. Many options exist to achieve this.

Process

Most IT service management practices revolve around process and this is where initial costs for adapting, planning and implementing them for your organization will occur.

CREATING AND DRIVING SERVICE EXCELLENCE

Products

IT service management tools are a hotbed market ripe with both good and bad advice. This is a topic of entire books! But a truth, no matter what tool you rely on, is that you will need tools. Automation of IT service management processes is a cornerstone of efficiency. There are large enterprise solutions and small niche products, all with merit. Prepare to budget for some level of tools costs. There are cost models that range from outright acquisition, lease, rent or open-source freely available, each with advantages and disadvantages. Use independent industry expertise if you need help to understand the choices and how they fit your needs.

Partners

One-time costs will be for contract negotiation, installation, and fee for service, integration and initial set up costs.

Additionally, one-time costs may be needed for process and product integration, testing and training.

Ongoing IT service management costs

People

Within any IT service management practice, people are your strongest asset. Ensuring they are trained, prepared and supported with the other 'P's' to carry out their role in delivering quality service requires an ongoing commitment. Rest assured that this investment is readily recovered in cost savings elsewhere such as less service disruption and fixing costs.

Process

Managing day-to-day process efficiency and effectiveness will have some program costs, many of which are covered within people, products and partners. One area, however, that needs attention is process improvement, which is needed to mature, evolve and keep processes current and aligned to business needs. This requires continual improvement analysis so the costs are associated to IT service management program reporting, analysis, improvement planning and then execution.

Products

Initial acquisition is generally the largest part of product costs over the lifecycle of a tool which is anywhere from 3 to 5 years on average. Ongoing costs include recurring licences, upgrades, maintenance and support costs.

Partners

These should be fairly minimal and related to internally driven changes to the IT service management program that must be aligned to partner products and services.

8 Return on Investment (ROI)

Most executives will look for tangible evidence that any investment they make will provide a reasonable ROI. This is just as true for IT service management. Earlier in this book, I provided some pretty attractive ROI estimates that organizations I have worked with and others have seen from adopting IT service management practices. We have already shown that there will be one-time and ongoing costs as part of an IT service management program.

The IT service management marketplace offers numerous tools, some free of charge for gathering the kind of information you need to calculate the ROI for IT service management. These tools basically operate on the same premise; you input some standard known current costs for such things as:

- Number of users
- Number of PC's and devices supported
- Number of services
- Annual IT budget
  - Capital and operational
- Number of incidents, changes, requests
- Number of IT staff
- Number of services supported

This is used in comparison to the ongoing costs which generally calculate savings based on such things as:

- Reduction in number of incidents
- Lower support costs
- Less downtime
- Lower costs per change, incidents
- Less unauthorized and failed changes
- Improved availability and reliability of services
- Improved productivity
- Lower risks to business

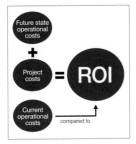

The tool then calculates, potential savings, establishes future ongoing costs and projects your ROI over a period of time, usually 1 to 5 years.

The following table (figure 6) shows some ROI for IT service management investment that may be helpful for ensuring you cover all areas when planning. This table uses arbitrary numbers intended to illustrate how ROI might look for your organization.

These costs are arbitrary for illustration, but are representative by ratio of ROI from industry norms.

In figure 6, we see that the use of IT service management can create savings in most areas of IT costs. Some savings are direct, such as those for reduced head-count, asset ownership, and support costs. Others are indirect but just as tangible to the business bottom line; reduced downtime, increased productivity; increased confidence in IT service, and higher rate of business change supported.

Projected savings from ITSM Implementation					
Cost item	Current	Year 1	Year 2	Year 3	Note
Infrastructure	40,000	32,000	20,000	5,000	Staged phase-out of hosting infrastructure from consolidation, virtualization cloud hosting. ITSM stability allows for more outsourcing control via supplier management and service performance monitoring
Facilities	300,000	300,000	200,000	150,000	Data centre no longer needed within 3 years
Human Resources	900,000	840,000	640,000	620,000	Some positions moved to oursourcer, others reduced through service consolidation and support rationalization
Licenses	60,000	45,000	42,000	42,000	Initial gain from unused license fees discovered, more outsourced hosting lowered internal software licensing need
Training	10,000	10,000	10,000	8,000	Initial ITSM training.
Security	25,000	25,000	20,000	10,000	Hosted service requiring less hands on supply due to implementation of internal security policy and practices.
Support	550,000	450,000	300,000	280,000	Includes – reductions in maintenance, upgrades, changes, requests, incidents, problems, etc.
Project Costs	0	800,000	300,000	100,000	Consulting, Tools, initial support, training for phased process implementation over 3 years
Projected savings	N/A	-617,000 (32%)	373,000 (20%)	760,000 (41%)	Savings from all budget areas as the result of ITSM. Some from lowered service disruption, some form new service architectures, some from lowered ongoing operational expenditures through process efficiency.

Figure 6 Sample projected savings for use of IT service management

The key to an accurate ROI rests in your organization's ability to accurately understand current costs, be realistic about the potential for savings and the time to achieve them, and using reliable ways to measure the outcomes at key points in time.

9   The same result but for a different reason

A good friend of mine makes a living in the IT service management world helping companies see how something unrelated to technology can make or break the success of service management. He decided that because he had to keep asking why we still have trouble being great at service management despite having every tool in the drawer at our disposal, that it was time to address the reasons why. He calls it ABC (Attitudes, Behaviours and Cultures).

I think it's important to mention here that there are a few things to remember regardless of what path you take to manage IT services:

- Your people are your greatest asset – or your most disruptive! No matter how advanced we become with technology, we will never replace the important role that people play in the customer's experience with service quality. The cultural ideals of your workforce toward service management must be embedded at every level in the organization to gain the optimal benefit

- We think of the cultural fabric within the IT organization as the Attitudes, Behaviours and Cultures (ABC's) we see every day, in every service encounter

- No amount of technology, process, procedure, work instruction, mandate, or management control, can replace the cultural acceptance and sense of value for IT service management within the workforce

- In order to be successful you need to treat a transformation of the ABCs as being as important as every other part of IT service management

10   Chiefly speaking

There is so much anecdotal information from IT service management experiences that it's hard to distil it all into meaningful advice. Here are a few pieces of advice that you might find helpful:

Beware of the IT service management zealot:

No doubt by now you have decided to adopt IT service management based on what you have read here, so you will go look for people to talk to about it. Every IT service management program needs its champions, but beware of those for whom the connection to official forms of industry best practice is more important than how it fits an organization. All IT service management frameworks require a moderate, realistic approach to adopting and adapting to local circumstances. Anyone telling you to go only by the 'book' is making false promises and you are wise to avoid such notions.

Once it's implemented the rest takes care of itself:

Many IT service management programs using this philosophy of 'implement and close', end up failing. IT service management is a practice with evolving knowledge and need and it is a living part of your IT organization. Considering it as such will ensure attention gets paid to its care and feeding just as you take care of servers, facilities, etc.

IT service management is an IT 'thing':

From planning to implementation and ongoing use of IT service management, those who consider it an IT thing, have missed the plot. IT service management is a business 'thing'. It might be seen most tangibly in operation within the IT organization, but be sure to realize that involving the business customer in all aspects of planning, use and measuring IT service management success will ensure you are doing the right things for the right reasons. Going faster in the wrong direction will just get you to the wrong place, faster!

Trust your instincts and use common sense is the best advice. If after having read this book you remain unconvinced that IT service management is an integral part of good business, then walk away because your efforts will fail without your commitment.

Chances are your managers and staff already know a lot of what you've read here. Now is the time to listen to their instincts and common sense. If that still isn't enough, step out of your office and look around at what your fellow IT executives are doing. You won't have to look far to find one using IT service management in your midst.

Remember that IT service management is common sense wrapped in the tried, tested and well-used experience of others. Use it, exploit it, adapt it and enjoy the rewards. Educate your workforce about IT service management by investing in content, knowledge and study. You will be on your way to joining the ranks of IT service management success stories and be respected by your customers.

Then get ready to be the IT executive the next reader of this book comes looking for advice from!

Appendix A

The following is a more detailed description of the IT service management frameworks mentioned in the Chapter entitled *'IT service management today'*.

Frameworks within the IT Governance layer

Standards

ISO 38500 – A standard for corporate governance of IT that defines six principles:

- Responsibility
- Strategy
- Acquisition
- Performance
- Conformance
- Human behaviour.

ISO 38500 provides a framework for effective governance of IT to assist those at the highest level of organizations to understand and fulfill their legal, regulatory, and ethical obligations in respect of their organizations.

Best Practices

COBIT[17] – A process-based governance and audit control framework. It is considered a management tool for developing governance and putting measurable, auditable controls into an IT organization.

COBIT is organized into four domains that cover various control areas:

- Planning and Organization
- Acquisition and Implementation
- Delivery and Support
- Monitoring and Auditing

COBIT will often be used in conjunction with the lifecycle management frameworks like ITIL, which are collaboratively mapped for use with each other.

Frameworks within the IT Strategy layer

Standards

INTERNATIONAL ORGANIZATION FOR STANDARDIZATION – ISO

ISO/IEC 20000 – Focused on IT service management, this standard has five parts:

1. Specification – This part promotes an integrated process approach to effectively deliver managed services. Co-ordinated integration and implementation of the service management processes provides ongoing control, greater efficiency and opportunities for continual improvement. The

---

17 Control Objective for Information Related Technology (COBIT), IT Governance Institute (ITGI), Information Systems and Control Association (ISACA).

specification draws a distinction between the best practices of processes, which are independent of organizational form or size and organizational names and structures

2. Code of practice – Depicts an industry consensus on guidance to auditors and offers assistance to service providers planning service improvements or to be audited against ISO/IEC 20000-1

3. Guidance on scope definition – Targeted to help service providers meet conformance of ISO/IEC 20000-1, or for service providers who are planning service improvements and intending to use ISO/IEC 20000 as a business goal

4. Process reference model – This describes the processes including the general service management system processes implied by ISO/IEC 20000-1. Each process of this model is described using a purpose and outcomes

5. Exemplar implementation plan – provides guidance to service providers on how to implement a service management system to fulfill the requirements of ISO/IEC 20000-1

ISO 27000 (series) – A set of standards exist within this series which specify the requirements for establishing, implementing, operating, monitoring, reviewing, maintaining and improving a documented Information Security Management System within the context of the organization's overall business risks. It specifies requirements for the implementation of security controls customized to the needs of individual organizations.

Further reference: www.iso.org

Best Practices

CONTROL OBJECTIVES FOR INFORMATION AND RELATED TECHNOLOGY – COBIT

COBIT's Plan and Organize domain – Provides guidance on having an IT strategy with an emphasis on business accountability and auditability. It nicely complements ITIL's guidance on formulating a service strategy (discussed next). COBIT's guidance ensures compliance to legislated mandates and audit controls, while ITIL provides guidance about how to create and maintain IT strategy for supporting the business services.

Further reference: www.isaca.org

ITIL SERVICE MANAGEMENT – ITIL

ITIL – A lifecycle-based set of practices supported by processes all focused on supporting business outcomes. Five core volumes of guidance depict each stage of the ITIL service lifecycle and the processes within them.

- Service Strategy
- Service Design
- Service Transition
- Service Operation
- Continual Service Improvement

ITIL best practices also contain complementary ITIL-based guidance on a wide range of special interest topics.

From an IT governance perspective, ITIL's Service Strategy lifecycle stage provides guidance for developing an IT strategy, creation of a service strategy, managing IT investments using a service Portfolio, and innovating service management through customer and market demand management.

Further reference: www.best-management-practice.com

Frameworks within the IT Management layer

Standards

ISO 19770 – Software Asset Management – Provides guidance to satisfy corporate governance requirements and ensure effective support for IT service management overall. ISO/IEC 19770-1:2006 is intended to align closely to and to support ISO/IEC 20000 (see IT governance section)

There are numerous other international standards that can fall into the IT management layer and which deal with the management of technical architectures, systems and information interfaces and artifacts. These will not be covered here.

Best Practices

Balanced Scorecard[18] – Provides a performance measurement tool for management for financial and non-financial metrics set against targets within four quadrants: Financial, Customer, Internal Business Processes and Learning and Growth. Its objective is to ensure proper organizational balance.

ITIL Service Design (SD) – Provides best practices in designing solutions to meet business needs, ensuring service capacity and demand are proactively embedded and the supply chain is planned and managed to exploit business benefits.

---

18   Kaplan R S and Norton D P (1992) "The balanced scorecard: measures that drive performance", *Harvard Business Review*

ITIL Service Transition (ST) – The next stage from Service Design in the ITIL service lifecycle, this volume deals with building, testing and moving services into live use for the business and how to manage the high risk activities of Change Management on an ongoing basis to minimize disruption and maximize stability.

ITIL Continual Service Improvement (CSI) – Used as an IT management tool, Continual Service Improvement best practices revolve around the other stages of the ITIL lifecycle and provide guidance for conducting performance assessments, benchmarking, service measurement and planning improvements.

Further reference: www.best-management-practice.com

CAPABILITY MATURITY MODEL INTEGRATION – CMMI

Developed by Carnegie Mellon University's Software Engineering Institute, CMMI is used for measuring process maturity against five levels of maturity and guiding organizations toward improved maturity and controls. It is a management tool that many organizations use on a recurring basis at established intervals to measure the effects of improvement initiatives such as those planned through the use of CSI.

Further Reference: www.sei.cmu.edu/cmmi/

Lean IT – Derived from the concepts of lean manufacturing in the early 1930's Lean IT has gained popularity in recent years as a management tool for better IT and business alignment through reducing non-value-added activities in the IT environment. Using exercises to create value-mapping streams, which identify how an activity adds value to the business and derives waste reduction, Lean IT follows a similar lifecycle approach.

Further reference: www.en.wikipedia.org/wiki/Lean_IT

THE OPEN FROUP ARCHITECTURE FRAMEWORK – TOGAF

TOGAF covers four types of architecture associated to enterprise IT architecture and describes these in relation to development aligned to business requirements.

Frameworks in the IT Execution layer

ITIL Service Operation (SO)– Part of ITIL best practices, SO deals with the ongoing daily processes and procedures for managing live services, facilities, teams and organizational structures associated with delivering and supporting live services. SO is both a management and operational layer tool but is best recognized in the technical operations areas of organizations.

Further reference: www.best-management-practice.com

Recommended further reading

If you want to explore more detail about various IT service management frameworks the following list will be helpful to access IT service management industry guidance.

ABC of ICT – An Introduction to the Attitude, Behaviour and Culture of ICT. Paul Wilkinson and Jan Schilt. Van Haren Publishing. ISBN 9789087531409

Frameworks for IT Management. Van Haren Publishing. ISBN 9789087531935

Tools for the Business When the Business is IT – Selecting and Implementing IT Service Management Tools. Robert Falkowitz. TSO (The Stationery Office) and itSMF International. ISBN 9780117069039

ISO/IEC 20000 – The Rise of a New Service Paradigm. Alex Hernandez. DragonFire Publishing. ISBN 10:0979235987

Leading Change. John P Cotter. Harvard Business Press. ISBN 0875847471

Business-Focused IT and Service Excellence. David Miller. BCS. ISBN 978-1-902505-88-6

World Class IT Service Delivery. Peter Wheatcroft. BCS. ISBN 978-1-902505-82-4

ITIL Lite: A Road Map to Full or Partial ITIL Implementation. Malcom Fry. TSO (The Stationery Office). ISBN 9780113312122

Changing the IT Leader's Mindset. Robina Chatham and Brian Sutton. IT Governance Publishing. ISBN 9781849280655

Enterprise Architecture as Strategy – Creating a Foundation for Business Execution. Jeanne W. Ross, Peter Weill, David C. Robertson. Harvard Business School Press. ISBN 1-59139-839-8

Service Management for Dummies. Judith Hurwitz, Robin Bloor, Marcia Kaufman, Fern Halper. Wiley Publishing Inc. ISBN 978-0-470-44058-2

The Executive's Guide to Maximizing strategic value from your IT investment. Dennis Ravenelle. TSO (The Stationery Office and itSMF International - coming soon

Service Intelligence –Improving Your Bottom Line with the Power of IT Service Management. Sharon Taylor. Prentice Hall. ISBN 10: 0132692074 , ISBN – 13: 9780132692076

Glossary

List of abbreviations

ABC	Attitudes, Behaviours and Cultures
CEO	Chief Executive Officer
ITIL	IT Infrastructure Library
ITSM	IT Service Management
ROI	Return on Investment
SO	Service Operation
OGC	Office for Government Commerce
PDCA	Plan, Do, Check, Act (Deming Cycle)
VOI	Value of Investment

Other books by Ms. Taylor:

ITIL V2 The business perspective;

(Contributing author); 2006, Office of Government Commerce

Publisher; TSO, The Stationery office

ISBN: 9780113308941

ITIL V2 – Small Scale Implementations;

(Co-author); 2006, Office of Government Commerce, Publisher; TSO, The Stationery office

ISBN:9780113309801

ITIL V3 – Service Management Practices

Service Strategy;

(Chief Architect); 2007, Office of Government Commerce,

Publisher; TSO, The Stationery office

ISBN: 9780113310456

Service Design;

(Chief Architect); 2007, Office of Government Commerce,

Publisher; TSO, The Stationery office

ISBN: 9780113310470

Service Transition;
(Chief Architect); 2007, Office of Government Commerce,

Publisher; TSO, The Stationery office

ISBN: 9780113310487

Service Operation;
(Chief Architect); 2007, Office of Government Commerce,

Publisher; TSO, The Stationery office

ISBN: 9780113310463

Continual Service Improvement;
(Chief Architect); 2007, Office of Government Commerce,

Publisher; TSO, The Stationery office

ISBN: 9780113310494

ITIL V3 – Introduction to the ITIL Service Lifecycle;
(Author) 2007, Office of Government Commerce,

Publisher; TSO, The Stationery office

ISBN: 9780113311316

ITIL V3 – Key Element Guides for Service Strategy, Design, Transition, Operation, Improvement
(Chief Architect); 2007, Office of Government Commerce,

Publisher; TSO, The Stationery office

ISBN: 97801133119, 20, 21, 22

ITIL V3 – Passing your Foundation Exam

First Edition (Chief Architect); 2007, Office of Government Commerce,

Publisher; TSO, The Stationery Office

ISBN: 9780113310791

ITIL v3 – Small-scale Implementation (Co-author);

2007, Office of Government Commerce,

Publisher; TSO, The Stationery office

ISBN: 9780113310784

Service Intelligence –Improving Your Bottom Line with the Power of IT Service Management, 2011 (Author)

Publisher: Prentice Hall

ISBN – 10: 0132692074

ISBN – 13: 9780132692076

For addition thought leadership by Ms. Taylor please visit www.aspect360.net

Many thanks to the following people who gave their time to reviewing this guide:

Dwight Kayto, PMP, FSM, ITIL V3 Expert , President, Art of Change

Vicente García , ITSMf Spain

Vince Lo Faso, Managing Director of IT service management, Navigo Technologies, LLC

Daniel Van den Hove – Alphega

Domitien Dijon – Demets&Heuskin

Todd Jarzinski, Global Client Services Manager, Telecom Industry

Joseph M. Bruno, Harvard University

Nevenka Cerovsky, Consultant, MKM d.o.o.

Antti Halila, itSMF Finland

Antonio Valle Salas – G2, Gobierno y Gestión de TI

Eric D'Souza, Harvard University

Paul Wilkinson, GamingWorks

INTERNATIONAL BEST PRACTICE

reening Service Management
e Relationship between Environmental
stainability and IT Service Management
hor: Ian Salvage with Karen Ferris

e industry commentators have stated that ITIL Version 3 missed
pportunity in not addressing one of today's biggest challenges -
ainability. This publication addresses that challenge and shows how
nisations can use service management to reduce the environmental
act of IT as well as reducing costs at the same time.

features include:
The Role of Governance - how and where does governance play a part
n achieving environmental change?
Where to Start - practical advice on how to make a start on addressing
he issues confronted by organisations
Measuring Environmental Performance - advice on measuring your
nvironmental performance.

l: 9780117068797
e: £35.00

IT Tools for the Business when the Business is IT
Selecting and Implementing Service Management Tools
Author: Robert Falkowitz

Very little has been written on the practices that should be adopted when
selecting and implementing software tools and most of it is from the
perspective of the processes that these tools support. This publication
will change that.

Key features include:
- The purpose and value of tools – what we can expect from ITSM tools
- Discussion concerning the architecture of IT service management
  systems
- A section on selecting ITSM tools, and the implementation of them.

ISBN: **9780117069039**
Price: **£50.00**

Notes

Notes

Notes